Published by Arrangement with R.S.Q. Phelps

First Printing, September, 2004

NEWPUB Books are published by
Phelps Publishing
16202 Spring Valley Road,
Piedmont, South Dakota, 57769

RAMBLINGS

The following pages are the ramblings of a bartender. I use the word 'bartender' very loosely because I'm really bad at the job. The traits necessary to be a good bartender seem to be lacking in my makeup. It would seem to me that the following attributes are the necessary requirements for a Jim-Dandy Bartender:

1. A good listener
2. A mixologist of high order
3. A memory for faces, names and drinks
4. An unyielding ability to keep opinions to him or her self
5. A repertoire of jokes several miles long

If a bartender has all of these attributes, they don't even have to be pretty or handsome (as the case may be). They just can't be unbearably or excruciatingly ugly. I suspect that my main problem as a bartender is that I just don't like the job. The reasons are fairly simple:

1. I'm not a good listener
2. If the name of the booze is not part of the name of the drink, don't ask!
3. I have to check my ID to see who I am, let alone remember who you are
4. My opinions are so important I must tell everyone ... and
5. I can't remember a joke more than two days

Having said all that, I own and tend a bar, needless to say, with limited clientele.

It was not my intentions to start a bar. I really was trying to build a golf course. I ran out of money so the Club House became a small bar. It is a 100-year-old barn. I have added a small extension or wing to it and have thus raised my seating from ten to twenty-two. Big Deal!

Being a college graduate with a wife of even higher intellect, we named the bar THE BARN. It seemed appropriate, somehow. Probably the only saving factor for our small business is my wife. She is very good at her job and is way more social than I.

Now, I must make something clear. I have said that I dislike bartending. I have not said I dislike our patrons. Actually, I find them delightful in their variety of lifestyles, intellect and personality. Over the several years that we have been in operation, I have met and enjoyed the company of many of our local people. Those that Edy and I like seem to keep coming back. Those that we don't...well they don't.

Many of our customers come with, or have been given, nicknames or monikers. For example, we have patrons called:

Fat Kat	Shut-Up Bob
London Marv	Rudy Three Times
Mr. Science	Mark the Old West Pro
Red Rover	Spidy
Slack	Glug & High Tower
Ronnie the Rip	SheepDog
Bradley the Leprechaun Biker	

And on and on, but you get the idea.

With each name, there is a story. Because we live in a small rural area, they seem unique to us. But they are not. I am sure that you can find these people in every small town in the Midwest. Still, *I sometimes suspect there is something wrong with our water!*

Over the four years of our operations, I have had the occasion to '86' only two people. One was for theft and one was for being alive! Every once in awhile, there is that individual of such obnoxious character that one has to wonder why someone hasn't dropped the hammer on him or her. Most people of that nature don't frequent our bar much more than once. Our regular customers can be quite cold and standoffish to that kid of person.

Even though I have fond feelings for 99% of our patrons, they can still get to me at times. When they do, I have to find ways to vent my feelings without insulting them. I also find that they do things that are quite funny or intriguing and I need to express my pleasure in some way. Therefore, I write. And that brings us to these ramblings and the reason for their existence. Let me tell you how this all started.

One evening, toward the end of the day, two couples came in for a drink or two. They were our only customers at the time and they were also new to the bar. As they sipped their drinks, one of the ladies noticed our Barn Animal signs hanging on the wall. These are wooden signs that have the name or nickname of one of our regular or special patrons carved on it. They sort of become a badge of identification and are a source of fun.

Anyway, the lady (a buxom red-head) says, "How can a person get a sign like that?"

I tell her that those are signs that I make for a few of our regular customers and they belong to me. I make them at no cost to the patron. She then asked that I carve her a sign. I told her that I wouldn't do that because she was not an established BARN ANIMAL and I didn't even know her name.

She continued to persist that I should carve a sign for her and finally I said, "Look, if you need to feel important, I will carve you one for $25.00." She said that would be great so I asked her what she wanted on the sign?

"Put 'Katie, That Sweet Irish Woman'", she said.

"That would take a sign over a foot long", I tell her. "Try something else."

"O.K.", she said. "How about 'Katie, That Sweet Irish Girl?'"

Exasperated, I threw up my hands and told her that I wouldn't carve her a sign. She laughed and over the next hour or so the foursome had a few more drinks and enjoyed themselves. During that time the redheaded Katie gave several ribald toasts that were quite funny and very well delivered.

The next day, while mowing the grass on our Driving Range, I got to thinking about "Katie, that sweet Irish girl" and her funny toasts. Over the next hour, while mowing, I wrote the following poem.

A Visitor To The Barn

This Irish lass walked into my place,
Sat down at the bar with a smile on her face
And asked if I would please take the trouble
To mix her a drink and, "Make it a double!"

"Well of course", say I, "for that's what I do,
Especially for girls as Irish as you."
For her eyes were sweet blue and her hair it was red
And t'was the sound of the Irish in all that she said.

A more innocent girl you'd never meet
For was clear she was gentle, kindly and sweet,
And as she knocked down the drink and started to pay...
Six of my patrons got in the way!

Three of them were married and two were quite old,
One was quite young, but exceptionally bold.
"Don't take her money", I heard them each say
It seemed that all six of them wanted to pay.

Gently she smiled and raised up her hand
And, when it got quiet, she told them how grand
That they were to treat her this way,
But it seemed quite unfair if only one were to pay.

She couldn't show favorites, that wouldn't be nice,
So each bought her a double poured over some ice.
"And now you must join me", she said with a grin,
"For the serious drinkin's about to begin!"

She raised up her glass and gave them a toast
And I must confess that it was probably the most
Ribald and funny that I'd ever heard.
I wish I could remember all of the words.

The boys at the bar laughed 'til they cried
And one of the old ones...Hell, he almost died!
The rest of my patrons all looked at each other
And loudly demanded she give them another.

She threw back a double (to quench her thirst)
And delivered another (as good as the first)
When the laughter subsided and they'd dried up their tears,
Commenced the biggest damn party I'd seen in six years...!

There was laughter and music and plenty of noise
And whoopin' and holler'en from the three married boys.
The two old ones were chasing some pretty gal
And the young one was trying to be everyone's pal.

I was busy a runnin' and serving away
When remember did I — t'was Saint Patty's Day!
I laughed to myself for, as you can recall,
It was a sweet Irish lass that started it all.

I turned to the spot where she had been sittin'
To ask of her name before I was forgettin'.
Her bar stool was empty, the Irish girl gone,
But she'd left a napkin that she'd written on.

"I know you're a wonderin' just who I might be...
I'm a sweet Irish girl by the name of Katie.
I was here for a purpose and I know I was bold
To totally ignore the Traditions of Old"

"So we honor Old Erin and Saint Patty's Day
And forgive my not takin' the traditional pay.
Some milk and some cookies might have been nice,
But I'd rather a Double, poured over some ice..."

Some time later, the redhead returned to our bar with a few of her friends. I saw her sitting outside on our patio and I hollered at her and said, "Hey, Katie. I've got something for you."

"Oh, you've carved me a sign", she said with a grin.

I walked out to her table, read her the poem, gave her the copy and said, "Now, don't ask me for no damn sign!"

She seemed to like it.

(Change of subject — that's why I called it *Ramblings*)

I have lived in this small community of Piedmont for many years and I will eventually die and be buried here. It is my home. Over these many years I have watched fellow community members come and go. A lot of people move to our area as a temporary stop in their lives and generally, as their situations get better, they move on. But there are others, like myself, that consider this to be home and, as the years roll by, I have watched a great many of them die, either from age, disease or accidental causes. In almost every case, it has been a loss to our community.

In February of 1999, a long time citizen of our area passed away. He was well into his eighties and had lived a full and quite productive life. He was a very good friend to my family and me and I will miss him always. Not long after, a Piedmont resident of 90 years also picked up his chips and cashed out of the game. The loss of these two long-time members of our small town got me to thinking about how much of a loss to our community the passing of these men were.

One has a tendency to view life from just in front of his or her nose. We seem to forget very quickly those friends and neighbors that share our lives and our times and then pass on. In just the few years that our little bar has been open to the public, several of our patrons have shuffled off this mortal plane and, even though we liked them and miss them, they come to mind only very seldom in some random remark or remembrance by one of our locals.

In thinking about this I started making a mental list of community members that had died in just the short time that we had been open as a bar and that led to the following poem.

Halloween At The Barn

Tending a bar is fairly mundane
And surprises are generally few.
Conversations are almost always the same
And so much that is said is not new.

Once in awhile, though seldom it seems,
That occurs which is worthy of note.
And over the years, serving thousands of beers,
Many stories a Tender could quote.

A case comes to mind, one I could tell.
Oh indeed, it did happen to me.
Though some time ago, I remember it well.
My memory is clear as can be.

T'was an October night, crispy and clear,
With fun costumes on my patrons all.
The liquor flowed free, as well as the beer,
As we enjoyed our Halloween Ball.

But most had to work the very next day
So quite early they started to leave.
Some of the guys still wanted to stay,
But the wives granted none a reprieve.

Prior to twelve, with all patrons gone,
I was setting alone in my Keep
Trying real hard to stifle a yawn,
But beginning to nod off to sleep.

At some point in time, I heard a noise
And it brought me straight up in my chair.
I must have dozed off and some of the boys
Had come in before I was aware

To my chagrin, as I looked around,
There were people all over the place.
Some that I knew from right here in town,
And then some unfamiliar of face.

Those that I knew were both neighbors and kin
And the strangers had names that I knew.
There was Vern and his Dad, Coob and Old Jim
And Vern Miner had brought his home brew.

They asked me questions, we talked and conversed,
They talked about their family or friend.
They asked bout the good things and questioned the worst
And left when the conversation would end.

It seemed sort of strange that I kept my head
As we talked the wee hours 'til dawn,
For I was aware...All these people were dead
Supposedly their souls had passed on.

Slowly they rose and started to leave
Their questions asked, answered and done.
And it seemed right they chose All Hallows Eve
For their night at the BARN and some fun.

Things then went cloudy. I woke with a start,
Confused but my memory clear.
Was it all real or was it just part
Of a dream and six bottles of beer?

Now was I asleep? Or was I awake?
Did this thing really happen to me?
Did my conscious mind make a mistake?
Did I merely just dream it to be?

I can't answer these questions, I must reply
But I await each Halloween with a chill.
The Graveyard lies upon a ridge nearby...
And it's just a short walk down the hill!

There were several other names I could have used in place of
Vernon, Coob, Jim or Vern Miner. It's sad that we so easily forget.

In the beginning of these ramblings of mine, I mention that one of the
drawbacks to me attaining the rank of good bartender is my tendency to
opine on any subject, especially politics. I am an avid follower of
politics in this great country of ours.

Its been said by many that politics and religion are not to be
discussed in a bar. I don't agree with all of that view. It is probably
right that religion might be better discussed in other than your local
pub, but not so politics.

There was once a time when most social intercourse took place in
either the church or the local pub and the general public was the better
for it. It must be remembered that the foundations of our nation were
set forth, discussed and debated extensively in the local pubs of the mid
1700's and from the pulpit of people like Patrick Henry. In this day
and age of lower literacy rates and educational deficiencies in the
general public, most people ignore politics and understand very little as
to the workings of our great nation.

Now I am a devout follower of politics and, during the Presidential political campaign of 2000, I made an effort to watch at least one of the debates between presidential candidates and the debates of their running mates. On the night that the Vice-Presidential nominees were to debate I told my wife that I was going home to watch it on TV, since I knew that it would not be welcome fare at the bar.

When I returned to the job, one of my regular customers asked me how I viewed the debate. At that point another of my customers got very hostile and began to rant about politics and how he didn't want to hear about it. He didn't care about the election process in any way and he was going to leave our establishment and not return until such time as the entire election was over and done!

Now this particular patron of our establishment, 'Shut-Up' Bob, is actually a pretty nice guy and I really like him. However, his action and words on that particular night struck me wrong and I was a bit put out at him. This man's major support was a government pension. His personal survival was in the hands of a government that he didn't even want to know about.

It was at that point that I looked at him and wondered why I liked him as much as I did. I had this thought that about the only thing that could like this man was a damn turkey, because they were just not that bright. I had this momentary vision of this stupid looking turkey with a big smile on its face. That vision led me to my next poem.

Before beginning my Thanksgiving poem, some background must be given about "Shut-Up' Bob. When they first meet the man, most people wish that he would "shut up'" or that he should be "shut up"! As you get to know the man, most people come to like him and enjoy his company.

Bob got into trouble with the law, when he was a young teenager, for some violent behavior and he did a little time. When he did something similar again, he was presented with the option of State-time or military-time. He opted for the military and stayed for 20 plus years. He did his time in Viet Nam and was the recipient of a few pieces of shrapnel, compliments of "Charlie". He loves explosives (from bullets to C4), believes in getting even and (this is the scary part) just doesn't give-a -damn!! Those are the ingredients of a dangerous man. Now to the poem:

Thanksgiving At The Barn
(Or A Turkey's Smile)

Did you ever see a turkey smile, especially in November?
If you ever saw a turkey smile t'was more likely in December!

Oh! Come On! You say. Don't give me grief. You know that's just a
pile!
With lips made rigid, it's beyond belief. Turkeys just can't smile.

Now what you say may well be true, but just listen to this yarn.
It's true what I'll be telling you, for it happened at the BARN.

It wasn't very long ago, with Thanksgiving drawing near
That my lovely wife decided we would do things new that year.

We'd still invite some friends to share our Thanksgiving dinner plate
But our turkey would be fresh that year, the best they ever ate.

So she bought a bird and brought it home, alive and doing great
Then we turned it loose so it could roam our yard from BARN to gate.

Now Turkeys aren't the smartest birds that ever graced the land
It's difficult to find good words, for I'm not their greatest fan

And dumb as turkeys well may be, this one also had a thing
Where t'wud strut around for all to see and crap on everything

A more obnoxious bird you'd never find, be you well assured
And Turkeyside would come to mind, just you say the word

I was not alone in the way I disliked this strutting oaf
Our patrons longed for the day it would became a turkey loaf.

All my patrons, save but for one, were all waiting for the day
When it was browned, basted, and all done and on the table lay

Oh! Sure this turkey was the worst but it a friend had found
A friend maybe even more perverse, but would never let it down.

When its friend objected to our plans for turkey day
It couldn't be expected that we'd change in any way.

So it really had no bearing on why we changed our plan
There's nothing wrong with sharing just dressing, yams and ham!

Did you ever see a turkey smile? Well, I think I did one time
When 'Shut-up Bob' looked up and said This 'Turks a friend of mine'!

By the way, 'Shut-Up' Bob did come back to the bar after the election was final. He looked at me, grinned and said, "I didn't think it would be this long!"

I have mentioned some of the nicknames of several of our customers, i.e. 'Shut-Up' Bob, Sheepdog, Spidy and others. It is necessary, at some point, to go into further detail of a few of these individuals. In that way, it will be easier to understand some of the poems I have written. A good example is the case of the Turkey's Smile and 'Shut-Up' Bob. One must know that he is (or could be) a dangerous man. Only in that way will the last line's significance be appreciated.

In the next poem, I write about the Christmas holiday. The poem is peopled with several of our patrons and alludes to certain characteristics of each that need to be explained. You have already become acquainted with 'Shut-Up' Bob so lets look at Spidy, Sheepdog, Mark and Bradley.

Spidy, though he appears normal in most respects, is one of those people that always seem to screw things up and, when he has an opinion, he is always right. (For example, "Snow is not water. It is crystals!)"

He became a local celebrity in our small town when he was written up in our area's largest newspaper. As one of our volunteer firemen, he was doing maintenance on one of the fire trucks and, with the truck's engine running, he decided to crawl underneath and check the transmission's shifting lever. The_header on the newspaper's article read...."Piedmont Fireman Runs Over Himself!"

"Sheepdog" Johnson came by his name for his love of telling dirty jokes in which the main characters include sheep. We have tried to get him to focus more on small dogs, chickens, donkeys or even humans, but so far to no avail. Don't misunderstand.... he is quite normal but we have fun with him and he plays along quite nicely.

Rich Bradley is a local biker who looks and dresses the part. He wears a small brimmed black leather hat on the front of which he has pinned a ceramic shamrock. He keeps his blond hair in a small ponytail and wears mustaches and a small goatee. He is small in stature and I have come to calling him a Leprechaun Biker.

Finally, there is Mark. Mark is a long time biker and has worked as a bartender for years. He has managed a very successful bar in Colorado. He is a big man with a full beard and wears black. Not only do you get the feeling that he has "been there and back" but he probably sold tickets. Mark has a sheer genius at getting his female bar customers to bear their breasts (which makes him extremely popular with male bar customers in the entire Black Hills area.) He has a couple of jokes that

he tells which end with him touching.... you know what I mean. Now
that the stage is set, here is:

The Barn Christmas List

Not so long ago a stranger stopped by.
He ordered a beer, then said with a sigh,
"This year is most gone and winter holds sway.
In just a few days, twill be Christmas Day."

All movement stopped dead—No one made a sound.
The poor guy looked up like some cornered hound.
Two patrons got slowly out of their seats
Then calmly they threw him out onto the street!

Now all of our customers aren't really that bad
And what happened to him was kind of sad
But...Let me tell you the reason for what had occurred
And I'll swear to the truth of every darn word!

Last year at this time, almost to the day,
Three people drove up on a strange looking sleigh,
A snowmobile painted deep red and black,
An old man a drivin' with two runts and a sack.

The old man was well dressed with white flowing beard
The runts were in greens looking generally weird
But I knew in a glance just who these guys were.
They were checking their list that was for sure!

From the time they drove up, it was like a curse.
It started out bad and quickly got worse!
For what and just who was the first thing they see?
"Hi there, old man. My name is Spidy."

"It sounds like your engine is missin' a bit...
So just stand aside and I'll quickly fix it."
"No, don't trouble yourself, for it is O.K.
We're perfectly happy it's running this way!"

Well, Spidy don't listen. He lies on the ground.
Reaches into the engine...Starts pokin' around.
"Get out of the way, you damn little Elf!"
Then moves a lever — and runs over himself.

You could see that the old guy was pretty well "pissed".
He took out a pad, then marked a name off his list.
Then he checked to see if Spidy had died
No, he was O.K., so they came inside.

They had a hard time finding a chair,
'Cause most of our crowd was already there.
There was 'Shut-up Bob' and his turkey friend
And Mark and Rich Bradley were down at the end.

One of the runts was female, it seems,
And pretty well stacked (if you know what I mean).
She sat down by Mark and I damn near choked,
When he started in telling her his old "Sweater" joke.

Well, I heard a slap and she stormed out of the door.
Was that bad enough?? Oh No..... there was more

Her diminutive friend by Bradley had sat.
He looked up and noticed Rich's black hat,
And seeing the Shamrock and beard like a goat,
His little eyes bulged and his face starts to bloat!

Now he gives Rich a look that could well have killed
And starts into cussing the 'Leprechaun's Guild'.
"The Irish are meddling where they shouldn't be
And this place is helping, that's plain to see!"

So, he takes out a pad, puts on some specs
And marks out a page with one great big "X"

Tween 'SheepDog' and Bob, the old man found a chair.
"Oh Lord", I mumble, "why must he sit there?"
The old guy turns white from something Bob said,
When 'SheepDog' starts talking, his face gets bright red.

Seems 'SheepDog' was in from his Montana run
Telling us all of his wild nights of fun
Driving the fence lines in the deep snow
Well, that was way more then we wanted to know!

The old man turned to me and shook his head.
It was plain there was nothing more to be said.
So laying his finger aside of his nose,
With quiet dispatch, from his bar stool he rose.

One thing I'll remember down through the ages.
As he walked out the door he tore out six pages
From that little pad he'd been thumbing through.
So much for Christmas! Not much I could do.

So my patrons are touchy this time of year,
And talk about Christmas they don't want to hear.
Not that Santa ignored us.... No, he played his role....
But just what do we do with this big pile of coal.

Sometimes things occur in our bar that needs to be recorded for the future generations of imbibers of adult beverages. Over the past several years there have been many such occurrences at the BARN. Some I have made note of and others need still to be written down for future reference. One such incident comes to mind.

The setting is a few weeks before Christmas. In one corner of our bar is a large box for toys being donated to needy children. Contained therein were such things as a soccer ball, a Tonka toy truck, a three foot tall Teddy Bear and various and sundry other items. As in most all bars, lying around was a couple of novelty items and some posted cartoons and jokes. As an example, one such item was a supposed can of rattlesnakes. When picked up, the can would start to rattle and shake. (Such sophisticated jokes just crack us up...!)

Into the above scene arrive the "Three Buddies" Riley, Denny and Jim. What follows is a fairly accurate account of what next occurred.

The Death Of A Legend

So you think the WEST is no longer WILD
And gone are the Injuns, Catamounts and Bear?
While I don't mean to scare no innocent child,
Here's a story that'll curl a bald man's hair!

Late one afternoon, as the sun sank low,
I saw them comin' down our dusty road.
When troubles a-foot—A Bartender just knows
So through my Bar door the 'Three Buddies' strode!

They slapped off the dust and each grabbed a stool
And with elegant grace, they slowly sat down.
T'was clear these three guys were totally COOL—
Tougher 'Men of the West' just couldn't be found.

Just who they were, all my customers knew
So they were careful to give em' their space...
And though they liked them, they followed the RULE—
"You don't ever spit in Superman's face!

Now Riley was beginning to worry,
As they stopped in for some after work beer
To make suppertime...he'd have to hurry,
But his Buddies said he'd nothing to fear!

"Be a Man", said his good buddy Denny
"Stand up and be free", said his buddy Jim
Now as for wives they neither had any
So what better people to advise him!

"Now women need Masters, someone who is firm.
Just like we dealt with our own, in the past.
We'll show her your not just some little worm.
We'll stand with you Buddy...right to the last!"

Boy, these guys are tough...that's plain to see
Ain't nobody shoves 'The Buddies' around!
Three brave men and bold, Denny, Jim and Riley,
With gonads you weigh by the pound!!

Now this is where things began to go wrong
To all of my patrons' awe and surprise
The fame of 'The Buddies' in legend and song
Started melting away right in front of their eyes!!

On top of our Bar a small box did reside
An unobtrusive and innocent thing
But holding a deadly object inside
Lying quiet and just waiting to spring

Riley decided to see how it worked,
For on its top was a door in a slide
With casual ease he gave it a jerk,
And it brought forth what was lying inside

It sprang out of that box like a bad dream
And crouched on the small door of its house
Riley gave forth a "blood-curdling" scream
From the threat...of the small plastic mouse!

Some patrons giggled and started to grin
And it caused one beer drinker to choke.
But steely-eyed glances from Denny and Jim
Made it plain they thought this was no joke.

To our Men's Room Riley then made his way,
While Jim looked for something to calm the man down.
It was about then that I heard Jim say,
"Hey Denny, you won't believe what I've found!"

"With this he'll cheer up," he said with a grin
Then he carried it to the Men's Room door
There are times 'Good Intentions' just don't win
There are times when things get worse than before

Jim holds up his find, as Riley steps out
Then he gives it a shake and whispers "Surprise"
I hear Riley gasp — and then a loud shout
Then he turns to jelly and crosses his eyes!

We couldn't contain our laughter and tears
And we all knew ridicule wasn't right
But I have to confess that in all of my years
I never knew Teddy Bears caused such fright.

Now the legend of three was down to just two,
But at least Denny and Jim were still MEN.
They were still guys with which you just never fool
Ooops! Then Riley's wife, she walks in!

All of this happened some time ago
When Molly came in and sat down
And when the dust cleared, wouldn't you know,
Those two brave men were nowhere to be found.

Now in our little town Legends die hard
Though at the BARN we try to keep them alive
As for the 'Three Buddies' they're always on guard
In FEAR that SHE might arrive!!

I fear I have bored you long enough so I will put an end to my
ramblings . . . for now. Our little area of the world is fairly dull and
quiet and there is not much exciting happening from day to day. Still,
I'm reminded of the love story and baffling mystery of "Latex and
Lime' or the time that 'Sheepdog' took his Montana vacation and what
about the Fourth of July antics of 'Shut-up Bob' and Rich 'the

Leprechaun' Bradley. Lets see...there was Deano 'the Beer Machine' and the hot clutch plate . . . and the twins and the magic appearance of a full moon on a moonless night . . . and . . .

I have not updated the happenings at the BARN since just before the Sturgis 2001 Rally and much has happened. Of course, none of it is in any way important. So let us see what is out there....

Edy and I look forward to each Rally. It's a lot of work and a bunch of hours but we get to meet some darn nice people over that 10-day period. Besides, we do rather well as to cash flow. That brings me to my next poem and the stupid actions of the businesses in our area.

Over the years I have watched as the local area businesses and the town of Sturgis have flailed away at the 'Goose' (the bikers) trying hard to knock loose a few more gold eggs. Greed has taken hold of most of the businesses that deal with the bikers, especially since the 50th anniversary. So here are my thoughts about the Rally (if not my thoughts, then my fears)

EXTRA!!! The Times EXTRA!!!

The Year That Nobody Came

STURGIS says:
"We don't understand...!!"

Hey Dad. Have you seen my Grandpa?
His old Harley is gone from the shed.
He'd not part with his bike less 'twas stolen
Or if maybe he fell over dead!

Now don't worry Son, for he is O.K.
The Old Man is out chasing his past
He's gone to a place called Sturgis
It's many years since he'd been there last

Where's Sturgis and why did he go?
Is Sturgis a long distance away?
It's a small town in South Dakota
And he'll have to ride back to yesterday

I know that sounds kind of funny
But you see, where he wants to go...
That town dried up next to nothing
Over twenty some years ago

Your Grandpa is old and he's lonely
To understand where he's gone, I'll explain
You see, he has lived to a fairly old age
And just a few of his old friends remain

Sturgis was where they would Rally
By the thousands and thousands they came
For a week your Grandpa would party
With at least two hundred friends he could name

A few Bikers gathered to ride and to race
When the Rally was first begun
And over the years it grew slowly
More than sixty-some years it would run

With each passing year the Rally got bigger
As more and more Bikers would ride
Through the late summer heat and their bike's pulsing beat
They rolled in like a great Golden Tide

As the Bikers rolled in, so did money
Arousing that monster named 'GREED'
And 'GREED' took control of poor Sturgis
Who decided on Bikers they'd feed

Raise prices on vendors and taxes
Gouge the Biker at every turn
More cops, harassment, and fines
Rip them off without a concern

Each year it got worse, never better
Rapacious 'GREED' was the name of the game
Raise a price here, collect a fine there
Get rich in a week was their aim.

Now they'd dealt with these Biker's for many a year
And you'd think they'd eventually learn
Those Bikers were damned independent
And for Fairness and Freedom they yearned

But Sturgis had forgotten the fable
Of that well-known Goose that laid gold
So blindly they plundered and pillaged
To the Bikers...it was getting damned old!

"Courtesy...Hell! Where's your money?"
"Fairness...Be Damned! Raise the price!"
"Five dollars more, just to get in the door?"
"It's three bucks for water with ice?"

Grandpa's friends started not coming
To this Rally they'd gone to for years
And Grandpa got fined three of four times
For drinking a couple of Beers!

It seems Sturgis had somehow forgotten
Why Bikers came back every year
Now the reasons they went to that Rally
Was for the Bikes and the Babes and the Beer

Now Bikers are use to harassment
From the cops and the places they ride
But push them too much with high prices and such
And they are gone like the outgoing tide

The last time Gramps went to Sturgis
He found all the streets wide and clear
Sturgis looked up and down and bewildered they found
Nobody came to the Rally that year!

Now the streets of Sturgis are quiet
Buildings with a 'CLOSED' sign on the door
On Main Street—three people and one mangy dog
And a sign reading
'BIKERS DON'T COME HERE NO MORE!!'

A Biker's memory is as long as a river
And they just don't forget over time
And though Gramps has gone back to Sturgis
He swears he won't spend one damn dime!

As the days, weeks, months and years go by, I seem to get no better
as a bartender. In fact, as the days piled up one after the other with
little if any time off, my patience and renowned good humor began
slipping. I found that I would use most any excuse to leave Edy behind

the bar and make my break for home. She is the more social of the two of us and seems to hold up much better than I do.

For some reason, as the Christmas season last year got closer and closer, I got more and more grumpy. I really don't know why. By the time the middle of December rolled around, I was seriously wondering what it would be like to just sell the place and find a small snug cave somewhere that I could hide in.

Then came our BARN Christmas party. It's an annual thing that we have been doing for several years and can be quite a lot of fun. Forty-two individuals showed up to participate in gift giving, sharing, and stealing from their bar-mates. As the night progressed, I had a couple of quite minutes to look around at the people who had come in to join the party.

If you have spent any length of time in your favorite bar or bars over several years, you will have found that there are always a few of the patrons that you would like to make go away...like permanent. Visions of mayhem and illegal activities cross your mind whenever you look at them. It doesn't make any difference whether you are a customer or bartender or owner, there are always several guys and at least one female that are on your secret 'Hit-List'. By the way, you are probably on several of theirs!

As I surveyed our Christmas party crowd, I caught myself with this goofy smirk on my face and it surprised me. Where was that grumpy bah-humbug Christmas attitude of the past several days? What was going on here? Then it hit me.

There were forty-two individuals, almost evenly split between male and female, enjoying themselves in a bar where I was both owner and bartender and... *I realized I liked every darn one of them!* O.K., that would warrant a smile of sorts, but why the smug feeling and the smirk?

The feeling of excessive self-satisfaction (*smug*) and the self-satisfied smile (*smirk*) came from realizing that those forty-two people were a compilation of all those hours, days, weeks, etc. of owning and running a very, very small bar (*a bar that just barely makes Edy and I a living*) and in many ways was a reflection on my wife and myself. These people certainly did not come to the BARN for the great bartending service or the grand and sumptuous surroundings. They came because they enjoyed the people and the atmosphere of the place and those are the reflections on Edy and I of which I speak. The smirk was because I knew that not very many bars in our area could boast of the same thing.

Needless to say, the rest of my Christmas season was better received by me and made coming to work over the next several months much easier.

I don't want to make it sound like we never have a customer or two (*or several*) that are not pleased with our establishment or with Edy or I. You are probably well aware that I take occasion to write a poem or two about our establishment and the on-going lives of some of our patrons. With just a touch of truth, a lot of salt and a generous helping of Bull, I write about our patrons and their supposed activities (most of which have never occurred).

In most instances, I "poke fun" at them but I try never to "make fun" of them. I think I know our patrons well enough to be able to judge whether they will be offended or not by what I write. But, of course, I am wrong. There is always someone who will not like what is said or written about them.

There is the case of 'Shut-Up Bob'. I really am quite fond of Bobbie and certainly would not purposely try to hurt his feelings...but it seems that I did just that with my Thanksgiving poem and my explanation of how I came to write it.

I wrote that Bobbie's "*sole support was a government pension...*" I was not demeaning him in any way with this statement, for the pension he receives is justly deserved from serving his country and doing so by placing his very life on the line. That is a great deal more than many pensioners can claim in earning their pensions. He viewed this statement as an insult and was not pleased, although I do not really know why. I have apologized to him but I don't know if that was enough from his point of view. But to set the record straight, I must add that he seems to have income from investments and labors that he does in building match-stick boxes, jewelry cases, (*quite good I might add!*), and other activities. Apology or no, I probably will not write about him again (*other than in passing*). I value his friendship and wish not to lose it with further aggravations

There is a couple that we alienated by our not giving enough free drinks or thanks for their patronage. We do not know if that is true. We have been told that was the case by friends of theirs but not by them...they refuse to talk to or associate with us.

When an individual got too much beer under his belt one evening and was a little to friendly with certain lady patrons, one of our bartenders cut him off for the night. He has not been back to the BARN since. More than a year and a half has passed since that episode. We assume that was the reason.

It never ceases to amaze me at what it is that will make some people mad and the way they handle it. Although this is probably not a valid assessment, it appears that people tend to get incensed over the most trivial things and at the same time will let the serious insults and grievances pass. 'Trivial Pursuit' is not only a game it also appears to be a way of life for many people. Not only do people react inappropriately to the trivial, they seem to delight in not talking about it to those they are mad at. One gets the impression that some people are just looking for the one little something that they can use to hold against others, that one little something that shows their superiority and the others inferiority. If they were to take their complaint to the offending individual or individuals, said problem might be cleared up and this would take away their claim to abuse from the ingrates of the world.

Thinking about that, I wrote the following:

It's All About Me

I awoke this morning to a world
That does not know my name
My morning mirror reflects a man
Who has no claim to fame

My wife has gone and left me
For some stupid ignorant jerk
With all her faults and him being dumb
It clearly will not work

I go to work each day late
And I leave it a bit early
I didn't get a raise in pay
So don't blame me for being surly

I was late for work again today
But the fault it wasn't mine
The damn law picked me up for speeding
And I stopped to pay the fine

I took a job this summer
A Bartender I would be
If the tip ain't big and the bribe not right
Hey, you get no booze from me

Come wintertime I quit my jobs.
Hell, it's cold that time of year
Pretend to look for work, collect my check
And order another beer

Some people say cut taxes
Quit picking' on the rich
That would make me work much longer
And that would be a bitch

The A-rabs killed some people
In New York you must remember
So with new extended benefits
I can quit as early as September

Life just ain't fair, that much is clear
And with my liberal sensibility
I must declare that all my mistakes
Are your responsibility!

If I were to die tomorrow
On my tombstone there should be
"I deserved way more than I received
From the world around me"

Now let's go back to that Christmas party that I mentioned above. I reread the poem the *BARN Christmas List* just before the Christmas party, 2001, and decided that I should really update our Christmas activities and maybe take some of the blame off of those individuals I had cited as culprits in the devastating Christmas of 2000. Now, I am sure that some of you are not aware of the letter we received from our North Pole friend and the events that followed. That being the case, you may catch up on our Christmas of 2001 by reading the following.

JOY TO THE BARN

It's Christmas time but you need not fear
Ain't like it was at the Barn last year
Our attitudes are a whole lot better
Since we received old Santa's letter

If you recall last Christmas season
For our bad mood, there was a reason
Santa dropped by to check on his list
And when he left he was damn well pissed

He tore our names from his Christmas Book
Sadly shook his head and off he took!
Well, we whined and begged and even cried
But that pile of coal is still outside

Christmas time will be better this year
And the BARN is filled with Yule Tide cheer
And to show you why, just let me quote
From that letter Mr. Santa wrote

In checking records from last season
It seems I felt there was good reason
For dropping you from my Christmas List
And Oh Yes, it's true. I was quite pissed.

Each new season I review my Book
And I now regret the steps I took
Though mistakes are seldom made by me
I must extend my apology

Mr. 'Shut-Up' Bob did quite offend
It was clear no one would call him 'Friend"
This I believed until just recent
When I found out the man's quite decent

And while it's true, he did offend
I was wrong—there's one who calls him "Friend"
"But it's just a Turkey!" my Elves all parrot
But where there's Love there must be Merit

And now for 'Sheep Dog, I must agree
I might well have judged him unfairly
He has spent this last year on the road
All across this land he's taken loads

And all those Montana escapades
In the deep snow and the Sheep Pen Raids
Have ceased it seems and he's now a pal
To a sweet and gracious Southern Gal

The Elves have said, "Santa, use you eyes!"
Sheep molestation is on the rise
I heard one whisper, "That stupid sucker"
"What about the Masked Phantom Trucker"

That female Elf that was well endowed
Of those mighty orbs is oft too proud
But said this of Mark, she would go back
And gladly face a frontal attack

If that is so, then how wrong was he
To touch and fondle those orbs of she
I see clearly now, my vision vaster
This Mark is truly a Titty Master

Now as to that Elf that carried on
About Rich Bradley, the "Leprechaun"
We checked their Guild and they said that he
Had been disbarred in eight-three

So the Elf was wrong in judgment there
And sadly admits he was unfair
To call him lout and stupid piker
When in truth he's just an old-time Biker

Not all the names that I rejected
Will be replaced as you expected
There is one that will not make the grade
For all the trouble that he had made

When we left your place and headed north
We were not worried so ventured forth
But soon our engine began to balk
For three hundred miles we had to walk

So we discussed it, the Elves and me
An answer to which we all agree
I have given Spidy a new goal
He'll be stopping by to pick up that coal.
SIGNED—Santa Claus

So, there you have it —it's all O.K.
Things are looking GOOD for Christmas Day
We'll all get presents and good cheer
And lift our glasses to the coming year!!

I see Kat and Ruth are acting up
And Mike and Dean are in their cups
Buford's in his Pirate mode
Giving forth his alphabetic code

Jersey has that look in her eye
And "Bite Me Buckoo" is her cry
When things can't get worse, who staggers in?
Your right! It's Riley, Denny and Jim

Ah, what the Hell. Things couldn't be better
Not after receiving Santa's Letter
But wait! Is that Santa pulling up out here???
My God! There goes Christmas for another year!!!!

After I wrote the above poem I felt a lot better. I had taken Mark, Rich, Craig "Sheepdog", and 'Shut-Up Bob' off the hook, so to speak. Then I realized I had just put Kat, Ruth, Dean, Mike, Buford, Jersey, and Denny, Jim, and Riley in the line of fire. Oh, Well!

Several years ago my wife's brother passed away from accidental cause and was buried in the National Cemetery about ten miles north of our town. Although Edy and I attended all of the services (at the church and at the National Cemetery service building), we had never been to his actual gravesite, so a couple of years later on Memorial Day we drove to the cemetery and spent about 20 minutes looking for her brother Vernon's headstone.

It was a cold and misty day with a fog settling down on the row after row after row of white headstones making the task of finding Vernon's gravesite difficult and miserable. We placed flowers on his grave (which the cemetery personnel remove within 24 to 48 hours) stood shivering for a few moments and then made our way back through the fog and white stone markers to our car. With our duty done, we drove back home and I opened up the bar. For me the experience was like the weather; cold, impersonal and depressing. All those hundreds and hundreds of markers made Vernon's grave seem insignificant and it was almost as though we were paying our respects to a white marker and not to the memory of Vernon.

I had not been open long when one of our local veterans came in looking wet and cold. He had been out doing what he did every Memorial Day, placing a small flag on his father's grave in the Piedmont Cemetery and paying his respects to those known and unknown veterans that had served our country in times of peace and in times of war. He was somewhat discouraged because very few people had shown up for the memorial service held by the American Legion at the cemetery. It was a day of remembrance and many had apparently forgotten.

I bought him a beer; he warmed his backside at the stove and went home. Later in the day, with no customers in the place, I got to thinking about that customer and his sincere feelings toward those men and women who had served our country and I compared it to my miserable and empty experience at the National Cemetery. Feeling a little ashamed at my lack of respect or regard for those individuals represented by those rows and rows of white markers, I wrote the following little story.

It was one of those miserable days of late May that you can get in this area. It just seems that *Memorial Day* is almost always wet and cold. I had made my trip to my Father's grave and set out my little American Flag to honor his service in our country's defense. With my 'duty' done, I drove back to the bar and opened for business.

The weather being what it was, the customer flow was sorely lacking...actually I sat there alone for a good 3 hours. It was just before dusk that I got my first customer. It was a man in his late 70's or mid 80's. He came in and sat down, wet from the miserable weather outside, and ordered two beers. I hadn't seen anyone come in with him, but I set up the beers as ordered and made with the general conversation.

"How's it going, friend? What are you doing out in this kind of weather?"

"Oh, I was just visiting my boy", he said, "and I thought I'd stop and buy him a beer."

I looked around and said, "I didn't see him come in with you. Did he go to the can?"

The old man looked up from his beer and smiled and said no, his son was not with him, and then commenced to tell me the following story. I will try to write it down like he told it.

I stood quiet and alone by a small tree engulfed in fog and lost in thirty years of memories. The day was cold with ground-hugging clouds and a misting rain. The gray damp fog turned a thousand simple white crosses into a double row of less than fifteen markers, with the second row fading into the enfolding fog, lending a feeling of finality to the scene.

Two middle-aged men were moving down the long rows, with a younger man seeming to follow with deference toward his companions. As their slow steps took them down the line, individual crosses would materialize out of the fog in front of them as crosses behind them disappeared. It was as though each marker was saying, "Here I am. Yes, I served my country. Remember me for what I gave. And let me not fade into the mist with distance and time." And then it passes from sight and a new cross appears ahead.

"Hey! Here he is."

Three men stood there, slumped into their coats for shelter from the wet and cold, yet still giving the impression of a respectful 'Attention'.

"I never knew him", the young one said.

"I was with him in Nam", said the man with the beard. The other man just nodded as, I suppose, memories of jungle green and the cold sweat of fear crossed his mind.

So, in silence they stood for a moment or two, each caught up in private memories, and then slowly they walked away. They left no flowers, none voiced a prayer, but as they disappeared into the fog I heard the bearded man say, "He was a damn good Man! Let's go get a Beer."

As I stepped out of the fog to the marker they'd just left, I realized that no flower or prayer or formal salute would have meant any more to the man in that grave than that parting remark of a fellow warrior. So, I stood for a moment looking at my son's marker, wiped some moisture from my brow and from under my eyes, then said "Son, let's go get a beer."

Memorial Day seems to mean a whole lot more to me these days since I talked to the warrior of WWII who bought his son a beer.

We do have a nominee for "quote-of-the-year-2002". It goes like this...

"All I can say is that I hate spics, niggers, Jews, and Catholics. I hate everybody. But most of all I hate a damn bigot!"

This quote came after several beers and a few shots of hard stuff (*and the guy tried to pretend he was serious*). The purveyor of the above wisdom has since moved away from our community. We have lost a good customer, a rather nice guy, and the wonder of seeing someone who could insert both feet into his mouth and still be able to talk out of the lower portion of his body. All kidding aside, Edy and I will miss him and his wife. They are very nice people.

Speaking of nice people brings to mind a certain Warren "The Hoofer" or, as he is known by some, "Mr. Latex and Lime". We at the BARN have tried for years to keep his story from the public. We protect our own and besides he is a good 'buddy' to Denny and Jim. However, Geraldo has been poking around trying to unearth all the particulars to this tale and, knowing how he seems to get most everything wrong, we have decided to set the record straight. (*By the way, I'm talking about Geraldo 'Clark Kent' Murphy who puts out a monthly newsletter in Tilford*).

The way the story has come down over the last few years is that the Latex and Lime incidents were simple acts of pranksters poking fun at Warren. The Latex side of the story has been told as that which follows.

It seems that some of Warren's close friends slipped up to his house unseen and tied a blow-up sex doll to his deck railing. When Warren came home that evening he brought some business associates and friends with him. As he came into the living room, he saw that his answering machine was indicating a message.

"We left a gift for you on your deck", whispered a voice.

How nice!

Excusing himself from his guests, Warren walked to the patio door, snapped on the light for the deck, and looked into the face of disaster — 'Matilda' the sex doll spread eagled and exposed!

My God! What would his guests think! This required quick action.

Warren snapped off the deck light, made some lame excuse to his guests about a chore he had to do outside, and slipped out onto the deck. He tried to quickly untie her from the railing but found that she had been cinched down with plastic ties. What to do?

Warren always carried a small knife with him that he used in his job related duties. He quickly took out the knife and began to saw at the plastic ties binding 'Matilda'. According to Warren, the lack of adequate lighting and his attempt to hurry caused his hand to slip and make a surgical-like slash in poor 'Matilda's' body. With the escape of air, Warren was able to extricate the wilted sex doll from its bindings and thus save himself from embarrassing ridicule from his friends and guests. So the story goes . . .

The second part of the Latex and Lime story begins just shortly after the 'Matilda' incident. Warren began to tell everyone how he hated the color Lime-Green. He made such a production out of it that one of his good friends threatened to sneak up to his house and paint his bridge that same putrid color. Of course, this was never done. Now here is the strange part.

There have been tales, from people passing Warren's house at night, that during a certain time of the summer Warren's bridge, from his house to his mailbox, seems to be wrapped in some sort of lime-green covering. Warren contends that some pranksters are sneaking up to his place and wrapping his bridge in a lime-green crepe paper. Mike, Buford, Denny, and Edy swear that this is not true. Oddly enough, this purported vandalism seems to take place on one particular night each year. It is almost as though it were an act of remembrance, an anniversary of sorts.

Now, from the archives of BARN lore, comes what some of us know to be the real story.

Latex and Lime

I'll tell you a story most shameful and gory
It's a tale of both pleasure and pain
Let me tell of a time known as *"Latex and Lime"*
It's a tale where dark madness does reign

When the day turns to dark and in some quiet park
Folks gather round a fire
And dark stories are told which makes the blood run cold
Of men most cruel and dire

The little girls quiver. The little boys shiver
And they all cover up their heads
Oh, they have a fun time until 'Latex and Lime'
That story fills them with dread

When ere this tale is told it seems one can behold
A shadow from a corner of the eye
And strange peals of laughter that echo long after
That shadow has passed quietly on by

Shush . . .Just Listen . . .
The night is softly rent by a moaning soft lament
Drifting faintly from the Ridge
Where covered in moonlight a dark shadow in the night
Stands mournful on his bridge

Now...
Young Matilda was a doll for which most men would fall
But Warren was the only one she wanted
She first saw him in her store where he bought books and something
more
Now her most private dreams he haunted

T'was then that her friend Vernon presented her to Warren
All inflated with the joy of this great day
For his love she was thirsting to the point of almost bursting
It seemed nothing could get in her love's way

With mouth so red and fair, lime green ribbons in her hair
Matilda was a vision of desire
To Warren's great surprise the invitation in her eyes
Had quickly set his yearning soul on fire

The social feelings of the day made it clear there was 'no way'
They'd accept such a deviant affair
One of Warren's greatest fears was rejection by his peers
A situation he simply could not bear

Though Matilda was quite pliant, Warren's attitude was defiant
Her affections cruelly he did spurn
But Matilda was not daunted and those private dreams he haunted
Only brought her passions to a burn

With the help of her friend Vern there was a way she might earn
The love that Warren left unrequited
If he saw her laying bare with green ribbons in her hair
He'd say "To Hell" with all his peers and be delighted

With arms stretched open wide to his railing she was tied
She knew he could not now refuse her
But to her sad despair when he saw her tied up there
To his shame, he started to abuse her

He said that she must go before his friends would know
That such as her was tied up at his house
"I want to see you nevermore. I must get you off the floor"
And "Oh, My God. Where are her panties and her blouse?"

He had some friends inside and there was nowhere he could hide
Matilda lying there tied up big as life
Though stirred with mad desire he tried hard to just untie her
Failing that—he pulled out his penknife

With his knife madly sawing and on those ties just barely gnawing
Clearly he'd not free her from the rail
Fearing his friends' derision he made a rash decision
Slashing out he thought he heard a soft wail

With a sighing sound of air he saw her wilting there
Her form distorting in the pale moonlight
And with shock he realized that right there before his eyes
His Matilda slipped quiet into the night

There's been many of a day that we've all heard Warren say
How he hates the color called *lime-green*
But hiding deep within his closet there he keeps on safe deposit
Two lime-green hair ribbons can be seen

Now the final irony, one for all the world to see
I saw one night as I drove past his Bridge
It was clearly wrapped all over with a *lime-green* paper cover
And I swore I heard soft laughter from the Ridge

The night is softly rent by a moaning soft lament
Drifting faintly, oh so faintly from the Ridge
Where covered in moonlight a dark shadow in the night
Stands with mournful laughter on his bridge

It is rather neat how a chain of events and thoughts can be traced to a certain action. As an example, consider the following:

1. Two customers commiserate with each other about their ex-wives
2. A lady wants me to carve her a Barn Animal Sign
3. An old Sci-Fi book title
4. A man and his wife from forty years in the past remembered.
5. The result of the above was another poem

The links of the chain began with two of our bar customers agonizing over their divorces and the resulting emotional and financial problems. In this business that Edy and I find ourselves in, we get to know quite a lot about those customers we serve. Several of our men customers are divorced, alone, and somewhat bitter. It is sad to hear about some of the things they go through in dealing with their ex-wives, greedy lawyers, and the State. This is not to say they were not responsible, in whole or in part, for the breakup of their marriages. It is only a reflection on their current condition.

An attractive lady named Kristel forged the second link of the chain. She came into our bar and decided that I should carve her a Barn Animal Sign. She made this demand on several different occasions until I told her that crying about it would not get me to carve the sign.

The third link in this chain of events was formed when I considered Kristel's persistent efforts to persuade. My reference to her 'crying' and that it would not help her to change my decision brought to mind the title of a science fiction book I had read, Nor Crystal Tears.

As I thought about the phrase 'crystal tears', I remembered a Naval Chief Petty Officer that I knew forty years ago. He was a timid man in a destructive marriage. It was a relationship with a woman who stripped him of his 'self-worth' at every opportunity. I liked him. I can only hope that one day he found he could stand up and say . . .

After All These Years

The sound of crystal laughter
Falls light upon my ear
A symphony of music
With each note crystal clear

To hear it from a distance
Did stir my yearning heart
Magnetic its attraction
It called me from the start

But crystal is the laughter
And each note crystal clean
With tension crystal shatters
Each crystal shard pristine

Directed in derision
Those shards can pierce the soul
And your use with such precision
Crystal laughter's beauty stole

Your laughter now breeds silence
And stillness in my breast
That helps heal my self-esteem
And allows my soul to rest

The sound of crystal laughter
So painful to my ear
Than the sympathetic beauty
Of falling crystal tears

The sadness as they shatter
Yet they end in strange delight
A warm chromatic rainbow of
Each tear's reflected light

The warmness of those crystals
As they burst in hues so bold
Are really quite deceptive
For each shard is crystal cold

Those crystal shards can cut you
To the bone and to the heart
And their multicolored beauty
Has torn my life apart

So the beauty of your sadness
Used so deftly through the years
Falls deaf upon my senses
So cry me no Crystal Tears

As I write this, I find myself wishing I had done so forty years ago
and had given it to the Chief. Neither was it written nor was it said. I
think of those two customers of mine and I lift my beer and say, "To
the Chief".

Another Christmas came along and once again the Barn customers screwed up a perfectly good holiday. I keep hoping that we can make it through a Christmas without aggravating Mr. Claus. As they say, Hope in one hand and …

We have two sisters that frequent our establishment as customers and occasionally as employees. One or both young women bartend for us during the Sturgis Bike Rally and at other times of the year. They have a tendency to not treat me with the dignity and respect I deserve so I decided to tell the story of our Christmas last. We are closed on Christmas and the following events occurred unobserved by any of our locals or Edy and I. However, even though both girls dispute our story, we got our information from a well-placed source in the Elf's Guild, Northern Division, Polar Sector.

Kristy and Lisa were kind enough to give Edy and I the night of Christmas Eve off. They said they would work that night and that we should have a nice night at home. We were quite pleased with their consideration for our family and us. Little did we know that they had ulterior motives.

Two Blonde Mice

T'was the night before Christmas
And the weather was nice
In a darkened far corner
Sat two little mice

One turned to the other
Said shouldn't we stop

Eating his cookies
And drinking his schnapps?

Now Sneaky just giggled
We've nothing to fear

Not after the way
He was treated last year!

But Santa had forgiven
The Barn and its crew
For screwing up Christmas
As they continually do

He showed up that evening
To their frightened surprise
Though fat and still jolly
A stern look in his eyes

And he punished them harshly
That much is true
Something mystical figures
Like Santa just do

"For eating my cookies
And drinking my schnapps...
OFF COME YOU TAILS
And he gave them a CHOP!

Well, there you have it
And I hope it's now clear
Why these tales are much shorter
Then the ones from last year

An occasional customer to the Barn is my brother Jim. He is a couple of years older than me and a great deal uglier. I have always felt a twinge of sympathy for him because he had to contend with a younger brother that had much finer attributes (such as better looks and a quicker mind) and mother loved me best. Sure, it is true that he has retired from a very good job and has a substantial retirement income and he has a million friends that think he is the funniest person they know and one of the smartest.

However, it must be remembered that almost all of these people are from western Nebraska, which helps to explain their confused thinking. Believe it or not, they even supported his run for Mayor of Crawford, Nebraska. It was his first venture into the realm of politics and, though he didn't win, the vote count was a dead heat tie. The election was decided by the flip of a coin, which Jim lost.

Not long after the election was over I was in Crawford and had occasion to speak to a few of the local residents. They had to tell me how Jim had almost won the election and how well he had done for a novice to the political profession. They went on and on and on. It became obvious something had to be done. These people were not aware of brother Jim's failings. My duty was clear. I went home to Piedmont and gave the problem some long hard thought. I wrote a letter to the Crawford Clipper newspaper and asked if they would print it on his birthday. They did. The people of his town are now much better informed and I feel that I have done my civic duty. Here is what I wrote. By the way, it was signed ANONYMOUS.

The Run From Mayor

Not long ago I was in your town
Where I met with a man called Jim
And as we talked people came 'round
He knew everyone and they knew him

I guess I was surprised to find
He had acquired some little fame
Jim had aspired to grand design
It seems he entered the politics game

For the job of Mayor he would run
As a novice this seemed quite a chore
Experience? Some thought he had none
But you see he'd run from Mayor before

To keep truth alive and set things straight
It's my duty this tale to tell
Of how he came to participate
In the mayoral run from hell

Some thirty years ago this race begun
In Arizona one Halloween night
When Jim decided to have some fun
As some Trick-and-Treaters came into sight

Now big Jim knew that there was nothing better
Than giving young kids a really good scare
If done right their pants would get wetter
And their little eyes cross in a blank stare

He grabs a sheet to throw over his head
Sneaks out the back door dressed like a ghost
They knocked on the door "Trick or Treat", they said
He laughs to himself, "These kids are TOAST"

Oooooh! He moans stepping into the light
Their mouths drop open and their eyes bug out
And cheery little faces all turn white
Silence! Then "RUN" somebody shouts

They all took off but one remained
In the dark stood this canine brute
With Toothy grin it was Hell Unchained
Jim in the lead; dog in pursuit

The dog had a name; they called him Mayor
Its only job to guard his Master
Lifting his sheet Jim saw this slayer
Started running but Mayor was faster

Jim with two legs the Mayor with four
It seemed not to be an equal race
Odds 2 to 1 he'd not reach the door
Before Mayor's teeth would end this chase

Now FEAR lends wings to a large man's feet
And Mayor hadn't run this hard in years
They might reach that door in a dead heat
Jim stretched it out, Mayor laid back his ears

Jim would have to slow to dive inside
And that darn Mayor was just too close
He couldn't afford to break his stride
He could feel hot breath from Mayor's nose

With barking dog and flapping' sheet
It's once more round the trailer boys
The thump ,thump, thump of tired feet
His wife's laughter over all the noise

Around the corner, head for the door
Decision made, its time to jump
Big Jim leaps and lets out a roar
Mayor is just inches from his rump

I never heard how this race turned out
Did big Jim make it safe inside?
Was his run from Mayor a total rout?
Are there little white scars on Jim's backside?

That first race from Mayor was long ago
He's never told me who wound up Boss
I guess if you really want to know
Call heads or tails give the coin a toss

I don't get to see my brother all that often but the same day the article was printed in his hometown newspaper he showed up at the Barn (a one hundred thirty-six mile drive). He accused me of writing this poem and I, being the kind of man that I am, denied everything.

My brother's birthday is in early May and we have a family reunion meeting at the Barn this year in mid June. That would have been a good place to post the *Run From Mayor* poem but Edy told me I couldn't do that. It's always nice to get a free shot at bother Jim but Edy is always right. However, even Edy makes mistakes. I've been waiting for better than thirty-four years for that first mistake and I know she will slip up sooner or later. Some of my friends say that she made a huge mistake more than thirty-four years ago but for the life of me I can't recall any such error in judgment.

The Hamaker Reunion (my Mother's family) went very well. Everyone seems to have had a great time and were pleased with The Barn and the way things were handled. It always surprises me on how shy most people are. Many of those who attended the reunion, rather than complement me directly, told Edy what a great job she did in getting things ready and how gracious she was to all those who came by. She told me later that she was quite sure they meant to mention me but were just being nice to her.

In about two weeks it will be the start of the 2004 Sturgis Rally. I have more to do than I can get done so I will end this addition to <u>Ramblings</u> and go back to work. I will have to get certain things out of my mind like the Wopahoe Tribe, "licking the dishes", the Ghost Of I-90 and . . .

The Rally is over and went well for us. Edy did breakfast for the Ralliers this year. It seemed to go well and I'm pretty sure she plans to do it again and better next year. If she would just slow down some, I am fairly sure my life would be a great deal easier. However, my character is such that I avoid at least 78.7% of the work and magnanimously let her make most of the decisions.

Dart season is upon us and we have several teams lined up to shoot in-house darts here at The Barn. That brings up a little episode that occurred not so very long ago and it should be related so that others might benefit from the story and avoid confrontation with certain CPA's.

(Begin truthful tale here:)

We, at the Barn, have had our run-ins with individuals of note. For example, we have sent bombs to Ben Laden via Afghanistan (with no return address, of course). The two thousand pound bombs with the legend "From the BARN with serious intent" could only be read on the way down and those who read it have since ceased to exist. We have dealt with Warren, the "Latex and Lime" guy, and have been confronted by Santa Clause for three years in a row. The 'Latex and Lime' guy knows that we still have evidence so he remains quite cordial. As for Santa, even when he is upset with us he is quite benign and we seem to be able to work out our differences each year.

The truth is that not all of our exchanges with the famous and infamous have been so risk free. There was one personage that gave me a cold chill and yet brought beads of sweat to my brow. Let me tell you how this came about.

This particular night started little different than the many others over the last ten years. The same customers were in attendance with a couple of newbies, as we call strangers. Phil and Marv were throwing darts with Trish, Squeek, Walt and Bueford. Phil had to deal with kids at the store all that day and was in a "lets kill em" mood and Buef was in his Pirate mode after several Rum & Cokes. Both were loud and Phil and Marv were stacking up points rather than closing out the game. Needless to say, the other players were getting a bit disgusted. Phil got louder and more boisterous and finally closed out at 760 points then proceeded to declare that they could beat anybody in the house.

Out of the corner of my eye I think I see a shimmering, like the waves of heat off an asphalt road, and I suddenly notice a man leaning against the wall next to the Barn Animal Signs. He is just leaning there, in his hand a long-stemmed Martini glass containing two large olives, while this little bat-winged imp perched on his shoulder and whispered something into his ear. This was damned strange. We don't have long-stemmed Martini glasses and I sure as hell wouldn't put *two large olives* in his drink.

With a small puff of smoke, the little imp disappears and . . .

Against the wall He leaned with ease
And a shadowed sneer curled his lip
I'll take that challenge if you please
From a stemmed glass he took a sip

Now just where in Hell he got that drink
With two olives in a yuppie glass
Couldn't help but make one think
As a Barn Animal he wouldn't pass

He says to the bar in a snake-like hiss
It shouldn't be much of a trick
In a jerk-water place such as this
To take two games from you small town hicks

Small town we are and hicks maybe so
We're nothing fancy but we're not low class
And as far as my Barn Animals go
It's who they are and you can kiss their . . .

The challenge could not be ignored. Phil did a little spin and said, "Bring it on, big guy". The first game of 301 was a rout. Phil was dead on and was out in just ten darts. The stranger threw like he had a broken arm and lost by an even one hundred points. Marv was in the game with only 74 points left but you could tell his enthusiasm for the game was gone.

Phil laughs and says, "That's one for the Hick!"
Buefs doin' the pirate's alphabet
The stranger gives his lips a lick
Sneers and whispers *"It ain't over yet"*

I smelled sulfur and the imp was back
He looked my way and gave me a wink
In his mouth a cigar, foul and black
Then he adds more gin to the stranger's drink

I knew this Imp from a time gone by
When I did my Thesis on the Necronomicon
I knew his name and that is why
I saw what other eyes could not focus on

Now it's not for me to interfere
In the games of chance that my patrons choose
But profit is the reason why I'm here
Can't have this imp serving his own damn booze

"Imp Azalyeh", I whisper low
And he looks up with an evil grin
"I have the power as you damn well know
So you best be losin' that devils gin"

Azalyeh glares then waves a claw
The gin bottle was gone in a burst of flame
He jerked back with a smoking paw
Then turned his attention to the new dart game

The education of the average youth in our society has declined to such an extent over the last few decades that I should explain a couple of things about 'familiars', imps and demons. The name of an individual familiar, imp, or demon is by which he or it is summoned. If you know their name and certain monstrous litanies, that individual can be called forth for whatever purpose you might have in mind. It's a risky business, for such things fight hard not to be controlled by a mere mortal. If you don't take care to have certain pentagrams or five concentric circles of fire coupled with the proper chants, you could end up as a puddle of black ooze or, even worse, living in a trailer house in Tilford.

Now it was obvious to me that this stranger, with the help of that damned imp, was setting Phil up for something but I couldn't figure just what he was after. Humans generally deal with imps for purposes of love or money. Nobody at our bar had huge amounts of money or was even heavy betters and love for Phil was out of the question.

> Phil tells the stranger, "You shoot first"
> Marv says, "I'm done. I'd rather drink"
> The stranger steps up with lips pursed
> The imp gives me a knowing wink
>
> The second game was owned by Phil
> His darts struck home without a miss
> But his game was not based on skill
> Each dart sped with an impish kiss
>
> The stranger's darts were off the mark
> By no more than a hole or two
> That imp would wave and change their arc
> Phil noticed not, he had no clue

Now those of you who know me are aware that I am quite observant and miss little that happens at my bar. I am not a great talker and I listen well. I only give advice when it is needed and I make it a practice to mind my own business and to not interfere in my patrons' personal or social lives. *(I also know that there is always that few who would strongly disagree with this accurate description of who I am.)*

It was clear to me that this stranger was setting Phil up for some nefarious purpose. What that purpose might be, I had no idea. It did seem odd that this stranger would employ an imp to help him lose a couple of games of darts in a small Piedmont bar. There was always a fairly heavy price to pay by any human that went to the effort to call up one of the denizens of the underworld. As I said before, I tend to mind my own business and I guess Phil was on his own.

The game ended with Phil "crowin' and a gloatin'" and the stranger making a big show of being mad as hell. The imp had done its disappearing act again (*I was getting a little tired of the puffs of smoke and the smell of sulfur*) and it was then that it dawned on me that something was more than a little strange between this Imp and his friend.

You see, calling up an imp is pretty much the same as calling a demon. Once you call them to you, they have a service or request to perform and then they are released. In other words, poof, they are gone. The major difference between Imp and Demon is that the demon has to be held kicking and screaming by inscribed pentagrams or such, whereas the Imp is employed for a price and needs no chains, incantations or artful means of capture to get it to do your bidding. If the price is right he stays, if not, another damn cloud of smoke and its gone. And that was the problem. This imp was bouncing in and out like a nervous lover. That just didn't fit normal behavior. About this time I began to suspect the truth.

> The stranger starts to make a scene
> He gripes about these stupid Hicks
> His words insulting and quite mean
> Phillip grins and calls him a dick

> *"Had I money"*, the stranger said
> *"I'd bet it all the next I'd win"*
> The Imp waves his paw, nods his head
> Another olive and more gin

> Now I had warned that Imp enough
> About my olives and that gin
> I guess t'was time that I got rough
> I had myself an Imp to skin

> But as I start to intervene
> Behind his back the man weaves a sign
> In a fiery hellish green
> And it sends a chill up my spine

> I hear Phil say as though compelled
> "Then bet your soul if you have no money"
> Then raucous laughter he expelled
> But I knew this wasn't funny

It finally added up. The Imp jumping in and out of real time, the stranger leading Phil on by losing dart games on purpose, the fact that he seemed to have inordinate control over the imp Azalyeh, and the final straw was his conjuring the "Compel" sign in Hell's own color. This was not a man. It was a demon and his very own pet imp.

I knew what was to come next and there was just nothing I could do to stop it. Oh, I could hold my own with an idiot imp but a demon was something else. With Phil gone, there goes another source of profit. Oh yeah, poor Phil.

> *"I'll bet my soul, if yours you'll bet"*
> The demon then its hand extends
> That's when my brow broke out in sweat
> It's now quite clear what it intends
>
> If Phil took the hand thus offered him
> The loss of his soul was the cost
> I must confess things looked darn grim
> If he touched that hand his soul was lost

Now I'm pretty easy going and, as I said before, I don't make it a habit to interfere in my customers' lives. However, this was going just to darn far. Not only was this imp stealing olives and pouring pilfered gin (I noticed my gin bottle's level getting smaller each time that imp filled the demon's glass), but he was also stinking up the place and flouting my warning. Even worse, the damn demon was about to take a good Barn Animal and turn him into a walking husk that probably would never tip again.

There was nothing I could do to stop the demon and prevent Phil from making this stupid bet. The demon's Compel Spell just couldn't be countered with the flick of the hand. It would take a strong incantation and the calling of the demon's name to break this spell and I had no clue as to who this demon was. But I could do something about that damned imp.

As Phil reached out his hand, I turned to Azalyeh and spoke. So much for the imp. Just then the side door opened with a bang and there stood Lance and Babbett Forrester (*of the East Coast Forresters, mind you*).

Lance stepped into the room right in between Phil and the demon and said, "Hey, have you guys heard the one about the insurance adjuster and the crazed North Dakotan?"

Little Babbett followed right behind and gave a 'princes wave' saying, "Hi guys!" She looked around with this sunny grin on her face and spotted the demon and his Martini glass. Now Babbett, when not flitting around in her upper social circles, passes time as a CPA and she can be quite insistent with those she serves as to cost saving measures. I have had to put up with her ragging on me far too long about the excessive use of large olives in our Bloody Mary drinks and in an occasional beer and I am not even one of her clients.

Phil tries to shake the demon's hand
But Lance stands firmly t'ween the two
Things not quite like the demon planned
His face takes on a greenish hue

Things tend to go "from bad to worse"
And that was just what happened here
He forgot all about his curse
When Babbett reached up and grabbed his ear

She hauled him over to the bar
And stared me sternly in the eye
"With these olives you've gone to far
And that Martini is way to dry"

Now that demon has had enough
Green fire leaps to weave a spell
He'd take no crap from this small fluff
He'd introduce Babbett to HELL

Damned if it didn't look as though I was about to lose another Barn customer. With a little work Phil could be replaced, but those east-coast Forresters were darn hard to come by. There was naught that I could do but watch the destruction of someone I had grown fond of. Besides she was right about the olives and her advise was free.

About then I noticed that all my other customers were all frozen in place like statues. Even the smoke from their cigarettes hung still and solid in the air.

She jerked his head down to her size
Then whispers something in his ear
A dazed look of complete surprise
Now what she said I couldn't hear

But then slowly the demon changed
The human clothes all disappeared
And the way his body was arranged
Grew green and bloated with lips sneered

The demon moaned, began to shrink
Down to near nothing' in less than a minute
Babbett reacted quick as a wink
Pulled a sack for her purse and stuffed him in it

The sack was gone in a puff of smoke and she turns to me as says, "Now Robert, I need to discuss our September Soirée."

I worked real hard to get my mouth closed back up and to assume a blasé attitude. I see the customers coming back to normal and its clear they saw nothing of what had just happened.

I turned back to Babbett and said, " Everything well be ready to go and your party should come off without a hitch." I couldn't hold back anymore so I asked, "O.K. girl, how did you get a handle on that demon?"

She grinned back at me and said, "Aw, handling simple demons is nothing, try dealing with an IRS agent sometime. By the way, that expensive toilet paper you are using in the bathroom . . ." Damn, now she's going to bug me about cheaper toilet paper!

And, yes, that ugly naked thing smoking that black cigar and doing dishes is Azalyeh, the imp. He'll be cleaning up around here for another thirty days and then I will give him his skin back.

My Uncle Larry Hamaker died. He was in his seventy's and his life was good. His passing reminded me just how much I liked him. It also leads in into my next little tale.

On a slow Sunday afternoon several of my customers and I were out on the BARN patio telling lies. Our conversation turned to people we had worked with over the years and the tricks we had played on them. There was the usual stories about sending a grunt to the shop for a 'spool of pipe thread' or to pick up a 'sky hook'. In truth, I never felt comfortable doing that kind of thing to a fellow worker or individual. That left me with nothing to tell, but then I thought of my mother's side of the family.

That whole family had the knack of 'story-telling' down to a fine art and a story that my Uncle Larry told me once came to mind. I told the story to my bar buddies and we got a laugh or two out of it but, I must confess, I could not do justice to the tale in the manner that my Uncle Larry could. His joy in telling the story and his enthusiasm and laughter brought as much to the story as the tale itself. The following written account will not come close to comparing to the 'leg-slapping, guffaw riddle delivery' of my Uncle Larry.

Carl and Rose Hamaker, my grandparents, lived on their home place in the panhandle of Nebraska where they ran a few cows and raised twelve children. They had some rough times and never really had anymore than 'just enough'. It was prior to and during the depression years and they were not the only ones living from hand to mouth. Still, they were better off than quite a few of the town's people. Although cash money was a scarce thing, with the summer garden, canning, and an occasional beef, there was plenty of food.

A couple of miles down the road they had a neighbor, for want of a name we will call him Henry, who was in about the same boat as they were. Now Henry and his wife didn't have any children and there were occasions when he would need help on his place and he would ask Carl if one of Carl's kids could give him a hand. That generally meant a few pennies in Carl's pocket or some kind of trade off, so Carl would send one of the boys over to help out.

There came a time when this neighbor decided to dig a well on his place so his cattle could get to water. In those days wells were dug by hand. Drilling rigs were expensive and hard to come by, so a shovel and bucket were the tools needed. Henry would dig down until he could no longer throw the dirt out of the hole and then another person was needed to pull up buckets of dirt and empty them to one side of the hole. That was where Uncle Larry came in. He was picked by granddad to help Henry dig his well.

The neighbor was a taciturn man. Not much to say and when he did say something it was usually gruff and short. He was a 'no nonsense' kind of guy and his wife was devoutly religious. They were a twosome, one pious in speech and both dour in attitude. It had been rumored that one of them had smiled a couple of years before and had regretted it ever since. Now contrast them with the Hamaker clan.

The Hamaker family consisted of fourteen people, Carl and Rose and the twelve children. In such a large family during hard times two things are almost always a necessity, a deep love of family and an abiding sense of humor. Granddad was king of all he surveyed, what little there was of it, and Grandmother was a mother, cook, doctor, and all-round fiddle player. Outside entertainment was a seldom, if ever, thing so all the kids played musical instruments of one kind or another and they all loved to dance. The twelve children all grew up with hand-me-down clothes and only lint in their pockets. If they had nothing else, all of them seemed to have a 'funny gene'. Almost anything they did or failed to do turned out funny. In the most dire circumstance or sad occasion, something would touch off their sense of humor and the giggles, guffaws, and leg slapping would commence.

My Uncle Larry was around thirteen years old at the time and he could work hard and was generally dependable, but neighbor Henry would have considered him irreverent and disrespectful of the seriousness of life. As far as Henry was concerned, by the age of twelve you put childish things, such as fun and laughter and music, aside and became a man.

Larry went each day for several days to Henry's place and they would walk about a short mile out to the well site to continue the well digging. Once the well was dug, Henry was planning to put up a windmill to pump the water into a large wooden stock tank.

They would start for the site around 6 AM and work until noon at which time Henry would tell Larry it was time for lunch. Henry's wife would make up sandwiches and a jug of milk and Larry would have to walk back to the house, pick up the food for Henry and himself and return to the work site.

On the first day of work Henry's wife brought lunch out to the well site. She made Henry and Larry sit through a long prayer to the Almighty before they could eat their sandwiches. After she had gone, Henry spent the rest of the day lecturing Larry on the futility of prayer. It seems that God didn't need to be begged for favors. If you were righteous in your life, God took care of His own. If you weren't, there was no need to beg, for Henry's God was not a forgiving God. His wife's noontime prayer wouldn't happen again. From that point on, Henry made sure that Larry walked to the house for the lunch. Since it was the only break Larry would get during the long day, he would trot to the house and take his sweet time walking back, lunch in hand.

While Larry was gone, Henry would continue to work in the well, digging and piling up dirt for Larry's return. With Larry gone, Henry would keep himself company by mumbling to himself about the inequities of life and all the things that had gone wrong over the last week or so.

On his return, Larry would lower a ladder down into the hole and Henry would climb out and they would eat their lunch. After about a thirty-minute break, Henry would go back down the ladder to resume his digging and Larry would remove the ladder to get it out of Henry's way. They would work until late in the afternoon then pick up their tools and head for home. Larry would get back home just in time for supper.

After spending the whole of the day with Henry, it was pure pleasure to come home to laughter, brothers and sisters, and music. Working with Henry was lower the bucket, pull up the dirt, lower the bucket, pull up the dirt and through it all not more than three whole sentences spoken by Henry from dawn to dusk, other than his monotone mumbling to himself. That was true unless Larry would let loose with a cuss word, a trait for which the Hamaker's were well known, and then it would be a ten minute lecture on the use of profanity in the eyes of God. By the fourth day Larry knew enough not to let any 'damn' or 'son-of-a bitch' slip out of his mouth.

Each morning the thirteen-year old knew he faced another totally boring day, but off he would trudge to Henry's place. It was on this fourth day, with the work almost done, that Larry's boredom got the best of him.

With the well hole more than ten feet deep, noontime came and Henry told Larry to head for the house for their lunch. Leaving Henry down in the hole, Larry was off at a fast trot.

As Uncle Larry came to the house, he noticed that 'Ole Blindee' was in the corral. 'Ole Blindee' was a blind horse of advanced age that Henry and his wife kept on the place. He wasn't good for much but they kept him fed and let him roam where he pleased. They would put a bell collar on him in the mornings and turn him loose. The bell on his collar would alert you to his whereabouts and you could keep track of his movements. It seemed that the misses hadn't turned him loose that morning and there he was in the corral with his bell collar hanging on the corral gatepost.

Larry picked up the sandwiches and milk jug and started back to the well site, but as he neared the corral a sly little grin crossed his face. Passing by the corral gate he grabs Blindee's bell collar and heads at a quick trot back to Henry and the well hole.

As he neared the well site, he slowed to a slow walk and lightly shook 'Ole Blindee's' bell collar. A tuneful "ding-ding" floated out into the quiet summer afternoon. With each step closer to the deep well hole Larry would lightly shake the bell collar. "Ding, ding-ding".

Now down in the hole Henry was digging away knowing that it would be another ten minutes before Larry was back with lunch. The dirt was beginning to pile up and in the eight-foot wide hole there wasn't much room to move around. At this point he always took a five to ten minute break and waited for Larry's return, all the while talking to himself about the harshness of life.

Larry was now less than fifty yards from the well, now forty yards, then twenty-five yards, and with each step or so he would gently shake the bell-collar.

"Ding, Ding, Ding-Ding", floated through the air.

As Larry approached the hole, he could hear the mumbled rantings from Henry deep down in the hole. It must have been about then that the soft, soothing, melodic sound of 'Ole Blindee's' bell began to register on Henry's ears. All sounds from the hole quit.

In the hole Henry could hear the bell getting louder and louder as 'Ole Blindee' got closer and closer. There was absolute quite from the well hole as Henry realized that that old blind horse was about to fall into the hole and on top of poor Henry. Larry was having a difficult time holding back his laughter.

Larry took several quick steps toward the well and shook the bell collar a couple of hard shakes; "ding, ding-Ding, DING". From the bottom of the well came a shaken and quiet "Whoa Blindee". Suppressing a giggle, Larry took a couple more steps and jiggled the collar.

"Ding, ding".

"Whooa Blindee", say Henry, his voice pleading and a little louder.
Larry was within just a few feet of the hole and with each step the bell rang its notes of doom. By this time, the taciturn, no-nonsense, naysayer of prayer had had enough.
"Oh God above! Holly Mary, Mother of God! Whoa Blindee, you son-of-o- bitch, WHOA!" So much for cussing and the futility of prayer.
It now dawns on thirteen-year-old Larry how much trouble he was now in. If the scared and rattled Henry ever found out that Larry was responsible for this, there would be pure hell to pay. Setting down the milk and sandwiches and holding the bell muffled against his chest, he ran full speed back toward the house and the corral. Placing the bell collar on the corral gatepost he was off again at full speed for the hole and the frightened Henry.
Arriving at the well site Larry hears nothing from the well and calls out that he was back with their lunch. A subdued voice comes from the well.
"Can you get that ladder in here right away?"
Crawling out of the hole, Henry looked all around.
"Have you seen 'Ole Blindee'?"
Keeping his eyes on the sandwiches as he unpacked them Larry says, "I think I saw him at the house, but I'm not sure".
They only worked a couple of more hours when Henry decided to call it an early day. It seems he wasn't feeling to good when he was down in that hole.
It was about fifty years later when Uncle Larry told me that story, slapping his leg and laughing from deep down in his belly. The contagion of his laughter and the way he delivered the story is something I will never forget.
I asked Uncle Larry, "Did Henry ever find out what you had done?"
"Nope. I don't think he even mentioned it to his wife. I think he figured it was just between him and God. For several years after that, Henry led a bible study class and a prayer group. It's kind of funny but every time I see that old movie with Jimmy Stewart, where they say that every time a bell rings an angel gets its wings, I think of Ole Blindee's bell-collar. Yep. Every time a bell rings old Henry says a prayer." Uncle Larry slapped his leg and gave out a big belly laugh and started telling the story of his grandson Brad trying to rope a rabbit.
That well got finished, 'Ole Blindee' finally expired, and they say Henry kept Blindee's bell-collar hanging on a wall next to a painting of two hands clasped in prayer.

It has been some time since I wrote anything down for this edition of *Ramblings*. As I write this last entry into this book, it is the first week of December 2005. My last entry herein is one that was meant for my wife. How much I miss her.

On March 17th of this year, 2005, our family got the devastating news that my wife Edy had lung cancer. According to the doctors, the situation was of a terminal nature and she was given only nine months to live. Their prognosis was fairly accurate and she passed away on the 20th of November.

I watched her get progressively worse day after day but the children and I tried to keep her hopes of survival up by avoiding the assumption of death. One must maintain hope and a positive attitude along with treatment, if one is to survive.

There comes a time when it becomes obvious that the chance of a cure or long-term survival is essentially gone. Although the family and I had reached that conclusion, she continued to have faith and fight. That situation made it difficult to tell her goodbye and of our deep love for her. It was at that point that I decided to try to tell her how I felt by writing her a story.

I told her of my intention and thought I might read it to her before the end came. It didn't work out that way. She passed away before I could finish and she was in a semi-conscious state during that last week of her life so I missed the opportunity to say a final goodbye.

The story that follows is my way of answering a question that Edy put to me a couple of times in the thirty-eight years we were together. When we were about to be married, she asked me if I minded being married by a Lutheran pastor. I told her that it would be fine and she then asked me, "What do you believe?"

Several years later, we decided to make a out a will to safe-guard our children in the case of our deaths. During the discussion she asked me again what I believed as to religion and death.

I never answered her questions, mainly because I was not sure then nor am I all that sure now, and I thought it might be a good time to give her an answer in those final days of her life.

Having said all of the above, Edy's story follows:

I BELIEVE

The full moon's bright light cast sharp shadows in the sacred circle of stones. This early in the spring of the year the nights were cool and the light breeze sucked away what little warmth the hooded cape provided. He followed in the footsteps of the old priest, with each step getting harder to take, as he approached the lone individual standing in the center of the Druid circle.

> The priest leads him through old Druid stones
> As those about him some chant intones
> Dread's cold hand slowed his stride

For on this night in this cold dark place
For the first time he'd come face to face
With one to be his bride

She stood silhouetted by a full moon, her dark hair stirring in the light breeze. The torchlight brought her face into view, strong features and straight lines softened by the warm colors of the fire. The young man's breath caught in his throat. This was no great beauty that he faced, but rather a simple peasant girl. Still, to him, all other women ceased to matter. She spoke. She smiled. He loved.

Silhouette carved by a full moon bright
Strong features soft from the warm torchlight
The young man caught his breath

He stood before her his heart ungloved
His soul soared upward. She smiled. He loved
Forever his 'til death

He held her hand as she lay dying and he thought back to that first time he saw her many years before. He had known from that first night that she was to be his forever. How short a time forever turned out to be. As her breathing stilled and her face softened from the lack of pain and life, his world turned gray and a light went out in his eyes.

The old man sat there softly crying
He held her hand as she lay dying
Forever he would grieve

As breathing stilled and Death took her soul
The light of his life Death also stole
Something whispers *Believe*

—Death is but a River—

His nose hurt and he could taste the blood as it flowed across his lips. The big boy sat astride his chest pinning his arms down with his knees. Another blow was being aimed at his swollen nose when a small hand reached in and grabbed a handful of hair on the big boy's head.

With a bloody nose and a swollen eye
But the big boy couldn't make him cry
Such was his stubborn pride

A voice irate "Let him up, you lout"
A small hand waves a big stick about
She could not be denied

The boys all scattered leaving him lying there with a dirty face and a
bloody nose. He was looking up at a mop of curly red hair and freckles
on a girl no bigger than a minute.

Red hair, freckles, and eyes a deep blue
A curious face that smiled at you
That face a pure delight

Her smile seemed to open up a door
That said they had met sometime before
On some long distant night

As he looked into her startling blue eyes, all the pain went away. All
of a sudden, everything was all right. In his short twelve years he had
never seen anyone prettier. He felt like he had known her forever.
"You better learn how to fight," she scolded

Her bright blue eyes took his pain away
Twas like going home to yesterday
Past visions dimly seen

"Learn to fight, whatever else you do"
He nodded. "Someday I'll fight for you"
A future unclear seen

For seven fine and full years the two were inseparable. Finally,
families had agreed and, with dowry offered and paid, the two were
married. The young man had grown to good size and was a respected
and valued fighting man of Waterford's town guard.

At nineteen years with a brand new wife
He answered the call of his Guard's fife
Strong her words as he departs

"Fight for our people and fight for me"
Pinned to his Jerkin for all to see
Her favor guards his heart

In that year of 1169 a small force under Raymond le Gros landed at Baginbun, near Bannow, and immediately routed a strong army of Irishmen and Norsemen from Waterford, inspiring the couplet:

> *"At the creek of Baginbun,*
> *Ireland was lost and won."*

He lay on the field of battle before Waterford. "Fight for our people. Fight for me", she had said. Now he would die for her. As his vision dimmed, his only regret was that he would never see her again. He whispers her name and the Irish monk beside him says, "Believe".

> He lay cold before the town's main gate
> Quiet, a hooded monk sits and waits
> As his life slips away

> His vision dims and he calls her name
> He breathes, "I'll never see her again"
> The monk begins to pray

> The monk bends close to the young man's ear
> "Be at peace my friend. There is naught to fear
> You have no need to grieve"

> The monk whispers, "There is no never
> Remember, death is just a river
> You simply must *Believe*"

As he slips into the lonely dark he seems to see a dark haired woman in a circle of stone and the smile of a redheaded lass. A look of content and he was gone.

> As the young man bleeds away life's spark
> And he slips into the lonely dark
> One last thing caught his eye

> He clearly sees with his final breath
> Something that warms the cold sting of death
> Then contented, he died

> A vision seen as through darkened glass
> The sweet smile of a redheaded lass
> And someone stood behind

Flickering torchlight with hair wind-blown
A dark haired woman, circle of stone
Somehow the two entwined

And dimly seen, a far distant shore
Where a lady waits with open door
She beckons from afar

'It's time to come home' she seems to say
'If you believe, you will find your way
Led by a sailor's star'

—On the River flows—

On the river of time the years and generations glide past. There one can see a collage of scenes that are years apart and seemingly unrelated.

She sits and waits on her cliff facing the sea for her man to come home his ship long overdue from its trip to the Americas. For many long years she waited; her love she'd not let go.
She sat alone on her bench each evening wrapped in her woolen shawl, as the sun dropped into the sea. Waiting, forever waiting, searching for the star that would guide her man home. The sound of the crashing surf and the breeze from the sea seems to whisper *'Believe'*
They found her there one morning, her twenty-three year vigil over, her waiting at an end.

I remember telling my mother, when I was but age ten, that I would not marry until I was thirty years old. I can still recall my solid conviction that this was true. I didn't know then why I was so sure of that statement. It was not until many years later that I began to think that I might know the answer as to the why of such a claim.
Through grade school, high school and several years after, I was not one to be comfortable around women. It was not that I was shy but rather I couldn't bring myself to participate in the social games the young played. It all seemed so shallow. It was as though I was looking for something or waiting for something to happen.

Twenty-seven years and still alone
Where his life was headed, still unknown
No goal for which to aim

With too much to drink, all night café
Occurred that which took his gloom away
Edy the lady's name

She took his order her gaze direct
Made something inside his mind connect
Vision briefly perceived

Darkhaired woman, redheaded lass
And other women from time long past
A distant voice *Believe*

So there is the story I said I would write for you. I have to apologize
for the fact that I cannot find an ending. The story remains unfinished
and I suspect that this is as it should be. You asked me once and twice
before just what did I believe. I tell you now, though you are not here
to hear,

He buried her on a winter's day
A part of his soul had gone away
Lowered into the ground

But he dreamed that night a dream most clear
One to soften grief and dry a tear
The lost seems always found

A dark haired woman stands proud behind
While up ahead and yet still to find
There awaits half his soul

—And On The River Flows—

www.ingramcontent.com/pod-product-compliance
Lightning Source LLC
Chambersburg PA
CBHW060616030426

42337CB00018B/3072